Nature's Fury

HURRICANES

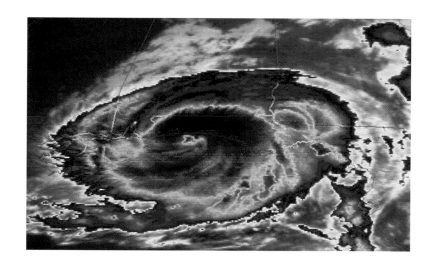

Cari Meister

Visit us at
www.abdopub.com

Published by ABDO Publishing Company, 4940 Viking Drive, Edina, MN 55435.
Copyright ©1999 by Abdo Consulting Group, Inc. International copyrights reserved in all countries. No part of this book may be reproduced in any form without written permission from the publisher.

Printed in the United States.

Edited by: Paul Joseph
Art Direction: John Hamilton
Contributing Editor: Morgan Hughes

Cover photo: AP/Wide World Photos
Interior photos: Digital Stock, pages 4, 5, 8, 26, 28, 31
                     AP/Wide World Photos, pages 13
                     Corbis, pages 3, 7, 8, 10, 11, 14, 15, 16, 20, 23, 27
                     National Oceanic & Atmospheric Administration, pages 9, 21, 22, 32
                     United States Air Force, pages 23, 24, 25

Sources: Dennis, Jerry. *It's Raining Frogs and Fishes: Four Seasons of Natural Phenomena and Oddities of the Sky.* New York: HarperCollins Publishers, 1992; Kahl, Jonathan D.W. *Storm Warning: Tornadoes and Hurricanes.* Minneapolis: Lerner Publications Company, 1993; Lane, Frank W. *The Violent Earth.* Topsfield, Massachusetts: Salem House, 1986; Laskin, David. *Braving the Elements: The Stormy History of American Weather.* New York: Doubleday, 1996; Various articles on http://www.usatoday.com. WEATHER section.

Library of Congress Cataloging–in–Publication Data

Meister, Cari.
    Hurricanes / Cari Meister
        p. cm. — (Nature's fury)
    Includes bibliographical references and index.
    Summary: Discusses the nature, causes, and dangers of hurricanes, hurricanes of the past, and ways to survive them.
    ISBN 1-57765-080-8
    1. Hurricanes—Juvenile literature. [1. Hurricanes] I. Title. II. Series: Meister, Cari. Nature's fury.
QC944.2.M45 1999
551.55 '2—dc21
                                 98-13130
                                     CIP
                                       AC

CONTENTS

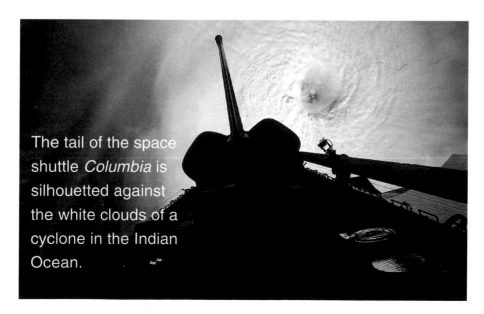

The tail of the space shuttle *Columbia* is silhouetted against the white clouds of a cyclone in the Indian Ocean.

HURRICANES

HURRICANES ARE CONSIDERED ONE OF NATURE'S MOST destructive storms. They bring heavy rains, fierce winds, and deadly waves. If a hurricane hits land, it is sure to leave its mark. Hurricanes rip up trees, destroy homes, and cause floods. Some hurricanes have killed thousands of people and caused millions of dollars in damage.

Tornadoes and hurricanes are both violent windstorms. Tornado winds are stronger than hurricane winds. Tornadoes are usually considered more violent. However, hurricanes are considered more destructive because they last much longer, and cover a much larger area of land. Tornadoes usually last under 15 minutes. Some hurricanes, however, last for three weeks. Tornadoes usually run a narrow path. But a hurricane can cover 500,000 square miles

Damage from Hurricane Andrew.

(1,295,000 square km) of land.

A hurricane is a swirling mass of thunderstorms. Some people think they look like big twisting tops, or giant snails. An average hurricane stretches 300 miles (483 km) across. Wind speeds inside hurricanes are usually around 100 to 200 miles per hour (161 to 322 kph). A hurricane is full of big, dark clouds. Inside a hurricane, thunder crackles and booms. Lightning lights up fierce clouds and rain pours.

A hurricane approaches the coast of Florida.

It's hard to believe, but near the center of the hurricane there is a spot where the winds are calm. This spot is called the eye. Inside the eye, the sky is sunny. A circle of storm clouds, called the eye wall, forms a ring around the eye.

Hurricanes form over warm parts of the ocean. Every sea in the tropics can spawn a hurricane. Most hurricanes start over the Atlantic Ocean, the Caribbean Sea and the Gulf of Mexico. Hurricanes usually form in August, September, and October. Meteorologists refer to this time as hurricane season.

Not all hurricanes hit land. In fact, most hurricanes remain out to sea. When hurricanes do come to land, watch out! Hurricanes can rip out piers. Hurricanes can flood towns. Hurricanes can turn a building into a pile of sticks. Every continent suffers the wrath of hurricanes, except for Antarctica. Hurricanes are most destructive on coastal areas.

Hurricanes have different names in different places around the world. The word "hurricane" comes from a word meaning "evil spirit." Long ago, people in the Caribbean believed that the evil god Huracan sent violent storms when he was angry. They believed that Huracan sent the storms to punish them. "Huracan" eventually became "hurricane."

In Australia hurricanes are called cyclones. A hurricane is a *cordonazo* in some parts of Mexico. *Cordonazo* means "lash of a whip." In India, a hurricane is called a typhoon.

Hurricanes cause a lot of destruction. But they are also an important part of the natural cycle. Hurricanes pick up water from the ocean. They often release the water back on land.

People everywhere depend on rain from hurricanes. Hurricanes and other tropical storms account for 10 to 15 percent of the rain that falls in the southeastern United States. Many farmers depend on hurricane rain. Their crops would die without it.

Hurricanes begin near the warm waters of the equator.

A satellite photo of Hurricane Elena, which passed over the Gulf of Mexico during the mid-1980s, shows the swirling pattern of the storm clouds.

Spin

Eye

FROM TROPICAL THUNDERSTORM TO HURRICANE

NEAR THE EQUATOR, OCEAN WATERS ARE VERY WARM. People come from all over the world to swim in tropical waters. Beware! Warm waters also breed deadly tropical thunderstorms and hurricanes.

A hurricane is a type of tropical thunderstorm. During a regular tropical thunderstorm, the wind picks up, the rain comes down, and big waves form. A hurricane is like a tropical thunderstorm, only much worse. During a hurricane, the wind rushes, the rain pours, and massive waves climb to great heights. Hurricanes are the most destructive of all tropical thunderstorms. All hurricanes develop from tropical thunderstorms. However, not all tropical thunderstorms develop into hurricanes.

Hurricane Andrew destroyed this man's home.

Tropical thunderstorms and hurricanes occur in the tropics during wet season. Tropical thunderstorms and hurricanes need two things: humid air and convergence. Humid air is heavy with water vapor. This occurs when warm air picks up warm ocean water. The warm air and water particles rise, making the air heavy and humid. When winds from opposite directions

8

Hurricane Fran threatens the Florida coast.

pound into each other, they pile up. Convergence is the coming together of these winds.

As more wind crashes into the pile, some of the air rises, which cools as it gets higher into the air. When the air cools, the water vapor in the air changes into rain, which falls back to earth. Is this a hurricane? Not yet. So far, it's just a tropical thunderstorm. Whether the storm becomes a hurricane depends on what happens next.

A tropical disturbance is the first sign that a hurricane may be on its way. A tropical disturbance occurs when a bunch of thunderstorms group together. The storm may stop there. It may never develop into anything worse. On the other hand, winds may start to swirl around and around. They may go faster and faster until a large vortex appears. If meteorologists confirm the wind speed to be 23 miles per hour (37 kph), the vortex

Winds of 100 miles per hour (161 kph) kick up waves in Biscayne Bay, Florida.

is called a tropical depression. If the winds swirl faster and faster and reach 40 miles per hour (64 kph), the storm is called a tropical storm. A storm is not a hurricane until wind speeds reach up to 74 miles per hour (119 kph). About one in every 10 tropical storms becomes a hurricane.

As a hurricane spins, it moves. The average hurricane moves about 10 to 50 miles per hour (16 to 80 kph). A hurricane can last for several days and travel hundreds of miles. Many hurricanes stay out at sea. Others attack coastal regions.

When a hurricane approaches, the skies turn dark. Thunder crashes. Rain pounds towards the ground. Winds blow fast, sometimes causing the rain to blow sideways.

A hurricane can cause a lot of damage. Some hurricanes bring so much rain that streets flood. It's common to see cars floating like boats. A hurricane's howling winds bend trees and buildings. Along the coast, huge waves crash against piers and beaches. Then all of a sudden, in the middle of the hurricane, there is calm. No wind. No rain. The sun is out. This is the eye of the storm. Watch out. The hurricane is not over. In time, the strong winds and rain will come back. They will come back just as powerful as before.

In 1988 Hurricane Gilbert produced enormous waves, which brought this Cuban fishing boat up onto the beach of Cancun, Mexico.

STRANGE, BUT TRUE

IMAGINE WALKING THROUGH YOUR HOUSE IN A FOOT OF water. You can't see where you are stepping. The water is muddy from the dirt that came in through the broken windows. Everything in the house is soaked in mud and water. Pictures, clothing, and furniture are ruined for good.

Maybe you find something floating in the water that doesn't belong. Objects sometimes travel from flooded house to flooded house in a hurricane. Everything is a mess. You feel awful. You think that nothing can be worse. But then you look out the window. Your neighbor's house is gone. The hurricane completely ripped the house apart. Only rocks and sticks remain.

Hurricanes are powerful, dangerous storms. They cause damage to human life and property both on shore, and at sea. Over the years, people have seen hurricanes destroy billions of dollars worth of goods. If you live near the coast, you may have seen the damage first hand. If you don't live near the coast, you probably have heard about it on television. But have you heard about the snake problem? Or the flying turtles? Hurricanes can cause some pretty strange stuff to happen.

In 1961, Hurricane Carla ravaged Texas City, with winds up to 145 miles per hour (233 kph). It rained so hard that the town flooded. Some people were able to get away before the hurricane hit. Others weren't as lucky. After the hurricane, the people who remained ran into another problem. Snakes! Snakes were everywhere. Thousands of rattlesnakes slithered through the town. Because the town was so flooded, the snakes went to the only high land. Guess who else was there? The hurricane survivors! The snake problem is fairly common in hurricane-prone areas.

In 1992 the winds of Hurricane Andrew were so strong they blew a piece of plywood right through this palm tree.

People have to be very careful in areas like Texas City, where some snakes are poisonous.

Wind gusts during a hurricane are very dangerous. You often hear about heavy objects whirling through the air, or about buildings blowing over. Sometimes hurricane winds blow over entire towns. But have you heard about the two flying turtles?

In 1935, two land turtles were caught in a hurricane. The turtles blew through the air for 20 miles (32 km). One turtle weighed 165 pounds (75kg)! They blew across the top of the Gulf of Florida. As they skidded across the water, they pulled in their heads and legs. Their hard shells protected them. Scientists were amazed the turtles lived.

Other hurricane survivors have witnessed some pretty strange stuff. Some hurricanes have ripped up graveyards. People have watched in horror as caskets floated down flooded roads!

Some hurricanes have even fooled Mother Nature. After some hurricanes, fruit trees and flowers have bloomed again, even though they were done for the year. Hurricanes can bring a lot of rain. When this happens, fruit trees get confused and think it's time to bloom again.

FAMOUS HURRICANES

TODAY, ALL HURRICANES ARE GIVEN HUMAN NAMES. Sometimes two hurricanes occur at the same time. By naming them, it is easier to talk about them and keep them apart. Hurricane names are chosen before the storms are even spotted. Every year a group of people comes up with a list of names before hurricane season. The hurricane names go in alphabetical order.

There is a list of names for hurricanes that start in the Atlantic Ocean. There is a list of names for hurricanes that start in the Pacific Ocean. The lists have an equal number of boy and girl names. For example, names for a year of hurricanes may start Axel, Bethany, Carl, Deb, Ernest. Hurricanes before 1979 did not follow this naming process.

Every year there are hurricanes. Some are worse than others. Over the years, some hurricanes have become famous. People usually remember the most destructive hurricanes. Therefore, the most famous hurricanes are usually the ones that caused the most destruction. People remember them because they were so horrible.

New England, 1938.

One of the worst hurricanes in history slammed into Bangladesh in November of 1970. Bangladesh is a coastal country in Asia. During the hurricane, 30-foot (9-m) waves

The hurricane of September 8, 1900, devastated Galveston, Texas.

came up on land. Areas of dry land became ravaging seas. The rain poured and poured, making the waters rise higher and higher. People did not have time to evacuate. Many people drowned. The official Bangladesh death toll was 300,000. More than a million farm animals died. Rice, the main food source, was washed away by the hurricane waters. Over 800,000 tons (725,744 metric tons) of rice washed away!

A devastating hurricane struck New England in September of 1938. The hurricane was named the "Long Island Express" because it quickly traveled up the East Coast. The Long Island Express flew up the coast at about 60 miles per hour (97 kph). The 180 mile-per-hour (290-kph) wind and rain destroyed many towns and claimed more than 600 lives. A pilot flew over the damage when the storm was over. He said this about the damage caused by the Long Island Express:

"Acres of trees were scattered about like matchsticks. Automobiles were lying on their sides, half buried in sand. Houses [mostly wooden] were flattened out as though they had been crushed under steamrollers. . . At one spot, nearly 15 houses were whirled together as though they had been in the grip of a giant eggbeater. . . Near Madison, Connecticut, there was the strangest sight of all—a two-story house which had been blown half a mile and had come to rest upside down without a single windowpane broken!"

In 1992, Hurricane Andrew devastated parts of Florida and Louisiana. Winds blew up to 165 miles per hour (266 kph). Ocean water poured into land. The water level rose 10 feet (3 m) above normal. Unlike the hurricane in Bangladesh, people knew that Hurricane Andrew was coming. People were able to evacuate. The death toll was small. The amount of destruction was not. In Florida, Andrew caused $20 billion worth of damage. In Louisiana, Andrew caused $300 million worth of damage. After the storm, people went back to look at their homes. For some people, nothing was left but a pile of rocks and sticks. For other people, their homes were standing, but they were flooded. Hurricane Andrew left about 300,000 people homeless.

The remains of Montego Bay, a neighborhood in Dade County, Florida, wrecked by Hurricane Andrew in 1992.

Songs from Dreamland

Songs from Dreamland

Original Lullabies by Lois Duncan

Illustrated by Kay Chorao

ALFRED A. KNOPF · NEW YORK

THIS IS A BORZOI BOOK PUBLISHED BY ALFRED A. KNOPF, INC.

Text copyright © 1989 by Lois Duncan and Robin Arquette
Illustrations copyright © 1989 by Kay Chorao
All rights reserved under International and Pan-American Copyright Conventions. Published
in the United States by Alfred A. Knopf, Inc., New York, and simultaneously in Canada by
Random House of Canada Limited, Toronto. Distributed by Random House, Inc., New York.

Manufactured in the United States of America   Book design by Mina Greenstein
1   3   5   7   9   10   8   6   4   2

Library of Congress Cataloging-in-Publication Data
Duncan, Lois, 1934–. Songs from dreamland : original lullabies / by Lois Duncan.   p.   cm.
Summary: An illustrated collection of lullabies and poems about sleep.   ISBN 0-394-89904-0
(trade) ISBN 0-394-99904-5 (lib. bdg.) ISBN 0-394-82862-3 (book-cassette)   1. Lullabies,
American.   2. Sleep—Juvenile poetry.   3. Children's poetry, American.   [1. Lullabies.
2. Sleep—Poetry.   3. American poetry.]   I. Chorao, Kay, ill.   II. Title.
PS3554.U464S66   1989   811′.54—dc19   88-21742

For Erin and Brittany Mahrer with love
—L.D. and R.A.

For Janet Schulman
—K.C.

WIND SONG

Wind at the window, sing us a silver song,
Silver as foam on an icy sea—
Silver as snow light,
Piercing the winter night,
Wind song and snow song for baby and me.

Wind song, silver song for us—
Sing it for baby and me.

Moon in the meadow, croon us a golden song,
Gold as the hum of the drowsy bees—
Gold as the moonlight,
Flooding the summer night,
Bee song and moon song for baby and me.

Moon song, golden song for us—
Sing it for baby and me.

Gold songs, silver songs for us—
Sing them for baby and me.

ROCKING CHAIR SONG

Somebody's baby is funny and fat—
Somebody's baby is naughty—
Somebody's baby got mad at the cat,
And somebody's baby is sorry for that.

Rock, rock–rock, rock—
Mother's rocking baby—
Rock, rock–rock, rock—
Mother's rocking baby.

Somebody's baby is bonny and bright—
Somebody's baby is funny—
Somebody's baby won't nap when it's light,
So somebody's baby gets cranky at night.

Rock, rock–rock, rock—
Mother's rocking baby—
Rock, rock–rock, rock—
Mother's rocking baby.

Somebody's baby is covered with crumbs—
Somebody's baby likes cookies—
Sooner or later the Sandman will come,
For somebody's baby is sucking a thumb.

Rock, rock–rock, rock—
Mother's rocking baby—
Rock, rock–rock, rock—
Mother's rocking baby.

WISH ON A STAR

Look out the window and wish on a star!
Wish on it quickly wherever you are.
Wish for the dream most important to you—
Wish, and that dream may come true.

Wish for a fuzzy warm kitten to hold.
Wish for a pony with hooves made of gold.
Wish for a necklace of sunbeams and dew—
Wish, and your dream may come true.

For the first star at night is a wondrous light
That is placed in the sky by the elves.
As it twinkles and gleams it can grant us our dreams,
As we know, for we've tried it ourselves—

Mommy and Daddy once wished on a star,
Wished on that magical light from afar,
Wished for a baby exactly like you—
See how our dream has come true!

THE SLEEPY SUN

When the sun is getting sleepy,
She slides down behind the trees,
Where she snuggles while she listens
To the singing of the breeze.
When my baby's getting sleepy,
He climbs up into my lap,
And he lets me sing him love songs
While he takes a little nap.

When the sun is very sleepy,
She slides down behind the hill,
Where she dozes in the shadows
While the world grows dark and still.
When my baby's very sleepy,
He leans back against my chest,
And he lets me hold and rock him
While he takes a little rest.

When the sun is *really* sleepy,
She slides down into the sea,
Where she dreams among the fishes
Of the day that's yet to be.
When my baby's *really* sleepy,
He falls fast asleep, and then,
He dreams of golden morning,
When the sun gets up again.

WHAT DID YOU DO TODAY?

What did you do today, little dog?
What did you do today?
"I went for a run on a rabbit trail.
I barked at the postman who brought the mail.
I yipped and I yapped, and I wagged my tail,
And that's what I did today."

Good night, little dog. Good night, little dog.
You have done everything right, little dog.
And now it is time to sleep tight, little dog,
For you've had a busy day.

What did you do today, little cat?
What did you do today?
"I purred so hard that my throat got sore.
I cleaned up a spill from the kitchen floor.
I got in a fight with the cat next door,
And that's what I did today."

Good night, little cat. Good night, little cat.
You have done everything right, little cat.
And now it is time to sleep tight, little cat,
For you've had a busy day.

What did you do today, little child?
What did you do today?
"I played in the car while we rode downtown.
I played in the park till the sun went down.
I played in the bath till the washrag drowned,
And that's what I did today."

Good night, little child. Good night, little child.
You have done everything right, little child.
Now I will snuggle you tight, little child,
For it's been a busy day.

TUCKING-IN SONG

Just one drink of water
Is all you will get.
With two drinks of water,
The bed might be wet.
With three drinks of water,
And one swallow more,
You'll find yourself swimming
Right out through the door.
So one drink of water—please, don't gulp that water—
One small cup of water, and not a drop more.

Just one bedtime story
Is all I will read.
For two bedtime stories
Are more than you need,
And three bedtime stories
Would take us all night;
We wouldn't be done
Till the sky filled with light.
So one bedtime story–one fairy-tale story–
One happy-end story, is all for tonight.

Just one good-night kiss
On the tip of your nose.
Then ten good-night kisses
On all of your toes.
A hundred more kisses
(That seems like so few),
There's just not enough
For a baby like you.
For kisses are different—and kisses are special—
And one good-night kiss—well, that just wouldn't do!

MOMMY'S TIRED TONIGHT

Baby, baby, loves to watch the moon,
Rising, rising, like a gold balloon.
Baby, baby, with your eyes so bright,
Close your eyes—close your eyes—
Mommy's tired tonight.

Baby, baby, loves the night bird's song,
Listens, listens, to it all night long.
Baby, baby, morning songs are best—
Go to sleep—go to sleep—
Mommy needs her rest.

Baby, baby, you've been changed and fed.
Baby, baby, see the pretty bed.
Hold your blankie, dream a happy dream—
If you don't go to sleep,
Mommy's going to scream.

Go to sleep—go to sleep—
Dream a happy dream.

DREAM ME AN APPLE TREE

Sleep, little child, and dream for me,
Dream me a white-plumed apple tree
All abloom in the early spring–
Dream me a song to sing.

Dream me a horse with a wild white mane,
Dream me a bird with a purple train,
Dream me a fish in a silken sea–
Dream me an apple tree.

Fresh from a land where dreams are made,
Tired child rests in a tree's cool shade,
Blossoms float in a silver stream—
Dream me a springtime dream.

Sleep, little child, and dream for me,
Dream me a house in an apple tree,
White lace ceiling and grass-green floor—
Dream me a child once more.

RED BIRD

Bright red bird on the branch above,
Hush your squawks and your "Peep, peep, peep."
Sing a song for the child I love—
Then fold your wings and sleep.

Brown-tailed squirrel in the maple tree,
Chat, chat, chattered till darkness fell.
Off you go with a one, two, three—
Sleep well, brown squirrel, sleep well.

For I know a child who played today
A little too hard and long,
And I know a child worn out from play—
That's why I sing this song.

Tired little head against my breast,
Soft little arms that cling so tight,
Time has come now to get some rest—
Good night, my love, good night.

THE RAIN LADY

Soft in the darkness the Rain Lady comes,
Twirling her hair with the tips of her thumbs—
Hair that is sweet as a summertime dream,
Studded with raindrops that sparkle and gleam,
Hair that is gray as the mists of the sea,
Whirling and swirling and tumbling free—
Shush, shush, don't make a sound—
Rest while the rain comes down.

Soft in the darkness the Rain Lady stands,
Shaking her hair with her gentle white hands.
Chipmunks and rabbits and ferrets and moles,
Tiny wet field mice run into their holes,
Sheep on the hillside and lambs on the plain,
Little wool blotters that soak up the rain—
Shush, shush, don't make a sound—
Rest while the rain comes down.

Soft in the darkness the Rain Lady sings,
Voice that is cool as the winds of the spring.
Rain in the leaves makes a whispering sound,
Light as the silk of the Rain Lady's gown.
Rain on the roof makes a patter like drums.
Soft in the darkness the Rain Lady comes—
Shush, shush, don't make a sound—
Rest while the rain comes down.

SLEEPY TOWN

Close your eyes–settle down–
That's how we get to Sleepy Town.
Close your eyes–settle down–
That's how we get to Sleepy Town.

Think of the wind blowing far and free,
Teasing the waves as it skims the sea.

Think of a meadow where silken grass
Bows to the wind as it hurries past.

Think of the birds in the autumn sky,
Sailing like kites when the wind goes by.

Think of the wind in the trees above,
Calling the name of the child I love.

Close your eyes—settle down—
Ride with the wind to Sleepy Town.
Close your eyes—settle down—
Ride with the wind to Sleepy Town.

THE TRAINS TO DREAMLAND

The first train bound for Dreamland
Is revving up to go.
See the sleepy passengers
Standing in a row.
Some of them are tall and thin,
Some of them are stout,
And see the silly baby
With his jammies wrongside out.

The first train bound for Dreamland
Is chugging down the track—
Mama will be waiting
When the train comes back.

The second train to Dreamland
Is standing at the gate.
See the sleepy passengers
Helping load the freight—
Baby dolls to cuddle with,
Teddy bears to pet,
And lots of fuzzy blankets
With their corners sopping wet.

The second train to Dreamland
Is chugging down the track—
Mama will be waiting
When the train comes back.

The last train bound for Dreamland
Is getting set to start.
See the sleepy passengers
Ready to depart.
Some are from the Northern Lands,
Some are from the South,
And see the silly baby
With her fingers in her mouth.

The last train bound for Dreamland
Is chugging down the track–
Mama will be waiting
When the train comes back.

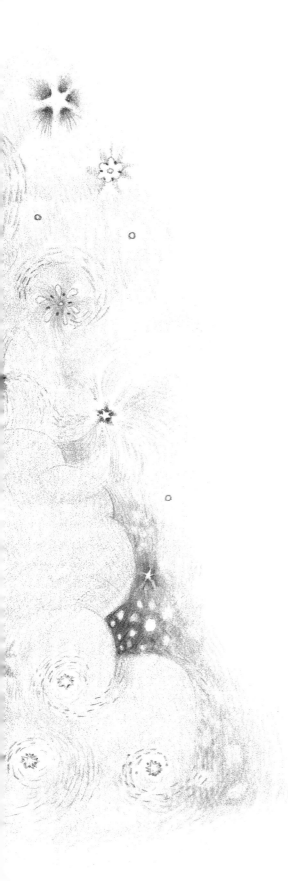

EVENING PRAYER

The beautiful day has slipped away,
And the night has moved gently in.
I kneel by my bed, and I offer thanks
For the wonderful time that has been,
For the song of the birds in the trees above
And the warmth of the golden sun.
I thank you, God, for your loving gift
Of the beautiful day that is done.

The beautiful night feels cool and right,
Now the warmth of the day is gone.
I kneel by my bed, and I offer thanks
For the wonderful hours till dawn,
For the crickets' song in the darkened hedge
While the stars fill the sky like flowers.
I thank you, God, for your loving gift
Of this beautiful night of ours.

SHIP IN THE NIGHT

Ship in the night–with salt in your sails–
Oh, what do you bring me from out of the deep?
"I bring you this wish from a magical fish–
Go to sleep. Go to sleep. Close your eyes. Go to sleep.
I bring you a comb that's frosted with foam,
A gift from a mermaid who wouldn't leave home,
And I'm bringing with me the song of the sea
To sing to the child that you love."

Ship in the night—with clouds in your sails—
Oh, what do you bring me from star-laden skies?
"A song that I heard from a magical bird—
Close your eyes. Close your eyes. Go to sleep. Close your eyes.
I've filled up my hold with gossamer gold
To weave you a blanket to keep out the cold,
And I bring you a tune I learned from the moon
To sing to the child that you love."

Lois Duncan, author of more than 30 novels for children and young adults, got the idea to write *Songs from Dreamland* when her first grandchild, Erin, who would not sleep at night, ran through the standard repertoire of "go-to-sleep" cassettes. Her eldest daughter, Robin Arquette, a professional singer and Erin's aunt, composed music to go with the lyrics. The lovely, lilting cassette *Songs from Dreamland* is the result of their collaboration.

Lois Duncan lives in Albuquerque, New Mexico, and Robin Arquette lives in Sarasota, Florida.

Kay Chorao is a fine painter who has written as well as illustrated many beautiful picture books. Her *The Baby's Lap Book, The Baby's Bedtime Book, The Baby's Good Morning Book,* and *The Baby's Storybook,* all of which are illustrated in a style similar to that of *Songs from Dreamland,* are considered outstanding books for the nursery-age child. She lives in New York City.

Songs from Dreamland

Songs from Dreamland

Original Lullabies by Lois Duncan

Illustrated by Kay Chorao

ALFRED A. KNOPF · NEW YORK

THIS IS A BORZOI BOOK PUBLISHED BY ALFRED A. KNOPF, INC.

Text copyright © 1989 by Lois Duncan and Robin Arquette
Illustrations copyright © 1989 by Kay Chorao

Manufactured in the United States of America   Book design by Mina Greenstein
1   3   5   7   9   10   8   6   4   2

Library of Congress Cataloging-in-Publication Data
Duncan, Lois, 1934–. Songs from dreamland : original lullabies / by Lois Duncan.   p.   cm.
Summary: An illustrated collection of lullabies and poems about sleep.   ISBN 0-394-89904-0
(trade) ISBN 0-394-99904-5 (lib. bdg.) ISBN 0-394-82862-3 (book-cassette)   1. Lullabies,
American.   2. Sleep—Juvenile poetry.   3. Children's poetry, American.   [1. Lullabies.
2. Sleep—Poetry.   3. American poetry.]   I. Chorao, Kay, ill.   II. Title.
PS3554.U464S66   1989   811′.54—dc19   88-21742

For Erin and Brittany Mahrer with love
—L.D. and R.A.

For Janet Schulman
—K.C.

WIND SONG

Wind at the window, sing us a silver song,
Silver as foam on an icy sea—
Silver as snow light,
Piercing the winter night,
Wind song and snow song for baby and me.

Wind song, silver song for us—
Sing it for baby and me.

Moon in the meadow, croon us a golden song,
Gold as the hum of the drowsy bees—
Gold as the moonlight,
Flooding the summer night,
Bee song and moon song for baby and me.

Moon song, golden song for us—
Sing it for baby and me.

Gold songs, silver songs for us—
Sing them for baby and me.

ROCKING CHAIR SONG

Somebody's baby is funny and fat—
Somebody's baby is naughty—
Somebody's baby got mad at the cat,
And somebody's baby is sorry for that.

Rock, rock—rock, rock—
Mother's rocking baby—
Rock, rock—rock, rock—
Mother's rocking baby.

Somebody's baby is bonny and bright—
Somebody's baby is funny—
Somebody's baby won't nap when it's light,
So somebody's baby gets cranky at night.

Rock, rock—rock, rock—
Mother's rocking baby—
Rock, rock—rock, rock—
Mother's rocking baby.

Somebody's baby is covered with crumbs—
Somebody's baby likes cookies—
Sooner or later the Sandman will come,
For somebody's baby is sucking a thumb.

Rock, rock—rock, rock—
Mother's rocking baby—
Rock, rock—rock, rock—
Mother's rocking baby.

WISH ON A STAR

Look out the window and wish on a star!
Wish on it quickly wherever you are.
Wish for the dream most important to you—
Wish, and that dream may come true.

Wish for a fuzzy warm kitten to hold.
Wish for a pony with hooves made of gold.
Wish for a necklace of sunbeams and dew—
Wish, and your dream may come true.

For the first star at night is a wondrous light
That is placed in the sky by the elves.
As it twinkles and gleams it can grant us our dreams,
As we know, for we've tried it ourselves—

Mommy and Daddy once wished on a star,
Wished on that magical light from afar,
Wished for a baby exactly like you—
See how our dream has come true!

THE SLEEPY SUN

When the sun is getting sleepy,
She slides down behind the trees,
Where she snuggles while she listens
To the singing of the breeze.
When my baby's getting sleepy,
He climbs up into my lap,
And he lets me sing him love songs
While he takes a little nap.

When the sun is very sleepy,
She slides down behind the hill,
Where she dozes in the shadows
While the world grows dark and still.
When my baby's very sleepy,
He leans back against my chest,
And he lets me hold and rock him
While he takes a little rest.

When the sun is *really* sleepy,
She slides down into the sea,
Where she dreams among the fishes
Of the day that's yet to be.
When my baby's *really* sleepy,
He falls fast asleep, and then,
He dreams of golden morning,
When the sun gets up again.

WHAT DID YOU DO TODAY?

What did you do today, little dog?
What did you do today?
"I went for a run on a rabbit trail.
I barked at the postman who brought the mail.
I yipped and I yapped, and I wagged my tail,
And that's what I did today."

Good night, little dog. Good night, little dog.
You have done everything right, little dog.
And now it is time to sleep tight, little dog,
For you've had a busy day.

What did you do today, little cat?
What did you do today?
"I purred so hard that my throat got sore.
I cleaned up a spill from the kitchen floor.
I got in a fight with the cat next door,
And that's what I did today."

Good night, little cat. Good night, little cat.
You have done everything right, little cat.
And now it is time to sleep tight, little cat,
For you've had a busy day.

What did you do today, little child?
What did you do today?
"I played in the car while we rode downtown.
I played in the park till the sun went down.
I played in the bath till the washrag drowned,
And that's what I did today."

Good night, little child. Good night, little child.
You have done everything right, little child.
Now I will snuggle you tight, little child,
For it's been a busy day.

TUCKING-IN SONG

Just one drink of water
Is all you will get.
With two drinks of water,
The bed might be wet.
With three drinks of water,
And one swallow more,
You'll find yourself swimming
Right out through the door.
So one drink of water—please, don't gulp that water—
One small cup of water, and not a drop more.

Just one bedtime story
Is all I will read.
For two bedtime stories
Are more than you need,
And three bedtime stories
Would take us all night;
We wouldn't be done
Till the sky filled with light.
So one bedtime story—one fairy-tale story—
One happy-end story, is all for tonight.

Just one good-night kiss
On the tip of your nose.
Then ten good-night kisses
On all of your toes.
A hundred more kisses
(That seems like so few),
There's just not enough
For a baby like you.
For kisses are different—and kisses are special—
And one good-night kiss—well, that just wouldn't do!

MOMMY'S TIRED TONIGHT

Baby, baby, loves to watch the moon,
Rising, rising, like a gold balloon.
Baby, baby, with your eyes so bright,
Close your eyes–close your eyes–
Mommy's tired tonight.

Baby, baby, loves the night bird's song,
Listens, listens, to it all night long.
Baby, baby, morning songs are best–
Go to sleep–go to sleep–
Mommy needs her rest.

Baby, baby, you've been changed and fed.
Baby, baby, see the pretty bed.
Hold your blankie, dream a happy dream–
If you don't go to sleep,
Mommy's going to scream.

Go to sleep–go to sleep–
Dream a happy dream.

DREAM ME AN APPLE TREE

Sleep, little child, and dream for me,
Dream me a white-plumed apple tree
All abloom in the early spring–
Dream me a song to sing.

Dream me a horse with a wild white mane,
Dream me a bird with a purple train,
Dream me a fish in a silken sea–
Dream me an apple tree.

Fresh from a land where dreams are made,
Tired child rests in a tree's cool shade,
Blossoms float in a silver stream—
Dream me a springtime dream.

Sleep, little child, and dream for me,
Dream me a house in an apple tree,
White lace ceiling and grass-green floor—
Dream me a child once more.

RED BIRD

Bright red bird on the branch above,
Hush your squawks and your "Peep, peep, peep."
Sing a song for the child I love—
Then fold your wings and sleep.

Brown-tailed squirrel in the maple tree,
Chat, chat, chattered till darkness fell.
Off you go with a one, two, three—
Sleep well, brown squirrel, sleep well.

For I know a child who played today
A little too hard and long,
And I know a child worn out from play—
That's why I sing this song.

Tired little head against my breast,
Soft little arms that cling so tight,
Time has come now to get some rest—
Good night, my love, good night.

THE RAIN LADY

Soft in the darkness the Rain Lady comes,
Twirling her hair with the tips of her thumbs—
Hair that is sweet as a summertime dream,
Studded with raindrops that sparkle and gleam,
Hair that is gray as the mists of the sea,
Whirling and swirling and tumbling free—
Shush, shush, don't make a sound—
Rest while the rain comes down.

Soft in the darkness the Rain Lady stands,
Shaking her hair with her gentle white hands.
Chipmunks and rabbits and ferrets and moles,
Tiny wet field mice run into their holes,
Sheep on the hillside and lambs on the plain,
Little wool blotters that soak up the rain—
Shush, shush, don't make a sound—
Rest while the rain comes down.

Soft in the darkness the Rain Lady sings,
Voice that is cool as the winds of the spring.
Rain in the leaves makes a whispering sound,
Light as the silk of the Rain Lady's gown.
Rain on the roof makes a patter like drums.
Soft in the darkness the Rain Lady comes—
Shush, shush, don't make a sound—
Rest while the rain comes down.

SLEEPY TOWN

Close your eyes—settle down—
That's how we get to Sleepy Town.
Close your eyes—settle down—
That's how we get to Sleepy Town.

Think of the wind blowing far and free,
Teasing the waves as it skims the sea.

Think of a meadow where silken grass
Bows to the wind as it hurries past.

Think of the birds in the autumn sky,
Sailing like kites when the wind goes by.

Think of the wind in the trees above,
Calling the name of the child I love.

Close your eyes–settle down–
Ride with the wind to Sleepy Town.
Close your eyes–settle down–
Ride with the wind to Sleepy Town.

THE TRAINS TO DREAMLAND

The first train bound for Dreamland
Is revving up to go.
See the sleepy passengers
Standing in a row.
Some of them are tall and thin,
Some of them are stout,
And see the silly baby
With his jammies wrongside out.

The first train bound for Dreamland
Is chugging down the track—
Mama will be waiting
When the train comes back.

The second train to Dreamland
Is standing at the gate.
See the sleepy passengers
Helping load the freight—
Baby dolls to cuddle with,
Teddy bears to pet,
And lots of fuzzy blankets
With their corners sopping wet.

The second train to Dreamland
Is chugging down the track—
Mama will be waiting
When the train comes back.

The last train bound for Dreamland
Is getting set to start.
See the sleepy passengers
Ready to depart.
Some are from the Northern Lands,
Some are from the South,
And see the silly baby
With her fingers in her mouth.

The last train bound for Dreamland
Is chugging down the track—
Mama will be waiting
When the train comes back.

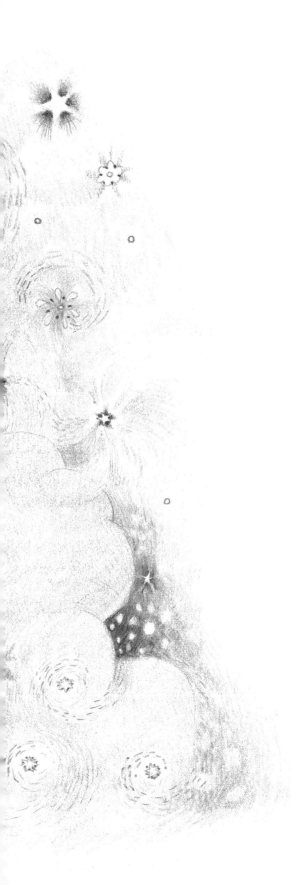

EVENING PRAYER

The beautiful day has slipped away,
And the night has moved gently in.
I kneel by my bed, and I offer thanks
For the wonderful time that has been,
For the song of the birds in the trees above
And the warmth of the golden sun.
I thank you, God, for your loving gift
Of the beautiful day that is done.

The beautiful night feels cool and right,
Now the warmth of the day is gone.
I kneel by my bed, and I offer thanks
For the wonderful hours till dawn,
For the crickets' song in the darkened hedge
While the stars fill the sky like flowers.
I thank you, God, for your loving gift
Of this beautiful night of ours.

SHIP IN THE NIGHT

Ship in the night–with salt in your sails–
Oh, what do you bring me from out of the deep?
"I bring you this wish from a magical fish–
Go to sleep. Go to sleep. Close your eyes. Go to sleep.
I bring you a comb that's frosted with foam,
A gift from a mermaid who wouldn't leave home,
And I'm bringing with me the song of the sea
To sing to the child that you love."

Ship in the night—with clouds in your sails—
Oh, what do you bring me from star-laden skies?
"A song that I heard from a magical bird—
Close your eyes. Close your eyes. Go to sleep. Close your eyes.
I've filled up my hold with gossamer gold
To weave you a blanket to keep out the cold,
And I bring you a tune I learned from the moon
To sing to the child that you love."

Lois Duncan, author of more than 30 novels for children and young adults, got the idea to write *Songs from Dreamland* when her first grandchild, Erin, who would not sleep at night, ran through the standard repertoire of "go-to-sleep" cassettes. Her eldest daughter, Robin Arquette, a professional singer and Erin's aunt, composed music to go with the lyrics. The lovely, lilting cassette *Songs from Dreamland* is the result of their collaboration.

Lois Duncan lives in Albuquerque, New Mexico, and Robin Arquette lives in Sarasota, Florida.

Kay Chorao is a fine painter who has written as well as illustrated many beautiful picture books. Her *The Baby's Lap Book, The Baby's Bedtime Book, The Baby's Good Morning Book,* and *The Baby's Storybook,* all of which are illustrated in a style similar to that of *Songs from Dreamland,* are considered outstanding books for the nursery-age child. She lives in New York City.

Songs from Dreamland

Songs from Dreamland

Original Lullabies by Lois Duncan

Illustrated by Kay Chorao

ALFRED A. KNOPF · NEW YORK

THIS IS A BORZOI BOOK PUBLISHED BY ALFRED A. KNOPF, INC.

Text copyright © 1989 by Lois Duncan and Robin Arquette
Illustrations copyright © 1989 by Kay Chorao
All rights reserved under International and Pan-American Copyright Conventions. Published
in the United States by Alfred A. Knopf, Inc., New York, and simultaneously in Canada by
Random House of Canada Limited, Toronto. Distributed by Random House, Inc., New York.

Manufactured in the United States of America   Book design by Mina Greenstein
1   3   5   7   9   10   8   6   4   2

Library of Congress Cataloging-in-Publication Data
Duncan, Lois, 1934–. Songs from dreamland : original lullabies / by Lois Duncan.   p.   cm.
Summary: An illustrated collection of lullabies and poems about sleep.   ISBN 0-394-89904-0
(trade) ISBN 0-394-99904-5 (lib. bdg.) ISBN 0-394-82862-3 (book-cassette)   1. Lullabies,
American.   2. Sleep—Juvenile poetry.   3. Children's poetry, American.   [1. Lullabies.
2. Sleep—Poetry.   3. American poetry.]   I. Chorao, Kay, ill.   II. Title.
PS3554.U464S66   1989   811′.54—dc19   88-21742

For Erin and Brittany Mahrer with love
—L.D. and R.A.

For Janet Schulman
—K.C.

WIND SONG

Wind at the window, sing us a silver song,
Silver as foam on an icy sea—
Silver as snow light,
Piercing the winter night,
Wind song and snow song for baby and me.

Wind song, silver song for us—
Sing it for baby and me.

Moon in the meadow, croon us a golden song,
Gold as the hum of the drowsy bees—
Gold as the moonlight,
Flooding the summer night,
Bee song and moon song for baby and me.

Moon song, golden song for us—
Sing it for baby and me.

Gold songs, silver songs for us—
Sing them for baby and me.

ROCKING CHAIR SONG

Somebody's baby is funny and fat—
Somebody's baby is naughty—
Somebody's baby got mad at the cat,
And somebody's baby is sorry for that.

Rock, rock–rock, rock—
Mother's rocking baby—
Rock, rock–rock, rock—
Mother's rocking baby.

Somebody's baby is bonny and bright—
Somebody's baby is funny—
Somebody's baby won't nap when it's light,
So somebody's baby gets cranky at night.

Rock, rock–rock, rock—
Mother's rocking baby—
Rock, rock–rock, rock—
Mother's rocking baby.

Somebody's baby is covered with crumbs—
Somebody's baby likes cookies—
Sooner or later the Sandman will come,
For somebody's baby is sucking a thumb.

Rock, rock–rock, rock—
Mother's rocking baby—
Rock, rock–rock, rock—
Mother's rocking baby.

WISH ON A STAR

Look out the window and wish on a star!
Wish on it quickly wherever you are.
Wish for the dream most important to you—
Wish, and that dream may come true.

Wish for a fuzzy warm kitten to hold.
Wish for a pony with hooves made of gold.
Wish for a necklace of sunbeams and dew—
Wish, and your dream may come true.

For the first star at night is a wondrous light
That is placed in the sky by the elves.
As it twinkles and gleams it can grant us our dreams,
As we know, for we've tried it ourselves—

Mommy and Daddy once wished on a star,
Wished on that magical light from afar,
Wished for a baby exactly like you—
See how our dream has come true!

THE SLEEPY SUN

When the sun is getting sleepy,
She slides down behind the trees,
Where she snuggles while she listens
To the singing of the breeze.
When my baby's getting sleepy,
He climbs up into my lap,
And he lets me sing him love songs
While he takes a little nap.

When the sun is very sleepy,
She slides down behind the hill,
Where she dozes in the shadows
While the world grows dark and still.
When my baby's very sleepy,
He leans back against my chest,
And he lets me hold and rock him
While he takes a little rest.

When the sun is *really* sleepy,
She slides down into the sea,
Where she dreams among the fishes
Of the day that's yet to be.
When my baby's *really* sleepy,
He falls fast asleep, and then,
He dreams of golden morning,
When the sun gets up again.

WHAT DID YOU DO TODAY?

What did you do today, little dog?
What did you do today?
"I went for a run on a rabbit trail.
I barked at the postman who brought the mail.
I yipped and I yapped, and I wagged my tail,
And that's what I did today."

Good night, little dog. Good night, little dog.
You have done everything right, little dog.
And now it is time to sleep tight, little dog,
For you've had a busy day.

What did you do today, little cat?
What did you do today?
"I purred so hard that my throat got sore.
I cleaned up a spill from the kitchen floor.
I got in a fight with the cat next door,
And that's what I did today."

Good night, little cat. Good night, little cat.
You have done everything right, little cat.
And now it is time to sleep tight, little cat,
For you've had a busy day.

What did you do today, little child?
What did you do today?
"I played in the car while we rode downtown.
I played in the park till the sun went down.
I played in the bath till the washrag drowned,
And that's what I did today."

Good night, little child. Good night, little child.
You have done everything right, little child.
Now I will snuggle you tight, little child,
For it's been a busy day.

TUCKING-IN SONG

Just one drink of water
Is all you will get.
With two drinks of water,
The bed might be wet.
With three drinks of water,
And one swallow more,
You'll find yourself swimming
Right out through the door.
So one drink of water—please, don't gulp that water—
One small cup of water, and not a drop more.

Just one bedtime story
Is all I will read.
For two bedtime stories
Are more than you need,
And three bedtime stories
Would take us all night;
We wouldn't be done
Till the sky filled with light.
So one bedtime story—one fairy-tale story—
One happy-end story, is all for tonight.

Just one good-night kiss
On the tip of your nose.
Then ten good-night kisses
On all of your toes.
A hundred more kisses
(That seems like so few),
There's just not enough
For a baby like you.
For kisses are different—and kisses are special—
And one good-night kiss—well, that just wouldn't do!

MOMMY'S TIRED TONIGHT

Baby, baby, loves to watch the moon,
Rising, rising, like a gold balloon.
Baby, baby, with your eyes so bright,
Close your eyes–close your eyes–
Mommy's tired tonight.

Baby, baby, loves the night bird's song,
Listens, listens, to it all night long.
Baby, baby, morning songs are best–
Go to sleep–go to sleep–
Mommy needs her rest.

Baby, baby, you've been changed and fed.
Baby, baby, see the pretty bed.
Hold your blankie, dream a happy dream–
If you don't go to sleep,
Mommy's going to scream.

Go to sleep–go to sleep–
Dream a happy dream.

DREAM ME AN APPLE TREE

Sleep, little child, and dream for me,
Dream me a white-plumed apple tree
All abloom in the early spring–
Dream me a song to sing.

Dream me a horse with a wild white mane,
Dream me a bird with a purple train,
Dream me a fish in a silken sea–
Dream me an apple tree.

Fresh from a land where dreams are made,
Tired child rests in a tree's cool shade,
Blossoms float in a silver stream—
Dream me a springtime dream.

Sleep, little child, and dream for me,
Dream me a house in an apple tree,
White lace ceiling and grass-green floor—
Dream me a child once more.

RED BIRD

Bright red bird on the branch above,
Hush your squawks and your "Peep, peep, peep."
Sing a song for the child I love—
Then fold your wings and sleep.

Brown-tailed squirrel in the maple tree,
Chat, chat, chattered till darkness fell.
Off you go with a one, two, three—
Sleep well, brown squirrel, sleep well.

For I know a child who played today
A little too hard and long,
And I know a child worn out from play—
That's why I sing this song.

Tired little head against my breast,
Soft little arms that cling so tight,
Time has come now to get some rest—
Good night, my love, good night.

THE RAIN LADY

Soft in the darkness the Rain Lady comes,
Twirling her hair with the tips of her thumbs—
Hair that is sweet as a summertime dream,
Studded with raindrops that sparkle and gleam,
Hair that is gray as the mists of the sea,
Whirling and swirling and tumbling free—
Shush, shush, don't make a sound—
Rest while the rain comes down.

Soft in the darkness the Rain Lady stands,
Shaking her hair with her gentle white hands.
Chipmunks and rabbits and ferrets and moles,
Tiny wet field mice run into their holes,
Sheep on the hillside and lambs on the plain,
Little wool blotters that soak up the rain—
Shush, shush, don't make a sound—
Rest while the rain comes down.

Soft in the darkness the Rain Lady sings,
Voice that is cool as the winds of the spring.
Rain in the leaves makes a whispering sound,
Light as the silk of the Rain Lady's gown.
Rain on the roof makes a patter like drums.
Soft in the darkness the Rain Lady comes—
Shush, shush, don't make a sound—
Rest while the rain comes down.

SLEEPY TOWN

Close your eyes—settle down—
That's how we get to Sleepy Town.
Close your eyes—settle down—
That's how we get to Sleepy Town.

Think of the wind blowing far and free,
Teasing the waves as it skims the sea.

Think of a meadow where silken grass
Bows to the wind as it hurries past.

Think of the birds in the autumn sky,
Sailing like kites when the wind goes by.

Think of the wind in the trees above,
Calling the name of the child I love.

Close your eyes–settle down–
Ride with the wind to Sleepy Town.
Close your eyes–settle down–
Ride with the wind to Sleepy Town.

THE TRAINS TO DREAMLAND

The first train bound for Dreamland
Is revving up to go.
See the sleepy passengers
Standing in a row.
Some of them are tall and thin,
Some of them are stout,
And see the silly baby
With his jammies wrongside out.

The first train bound for Dreamland
Is chugging down the track—
Mama will be waiting
When the train comes back.

The second train to Dreamland
Is standing at the gate.
See the sleepy passengers
Helping load the freight—
Baby dolls to cuddle with,
Teddy bears to pet,
And lots of fuzzy blankets
With their corners sopping wet.

The second train to Dreamland
Is chugging down the track—
Mama will be waiting
When the train comes back.

Songs from Dreamland

Songs from Dreamland

Original Lullabies by Lois Duncan

Illustrated by Kay Chorao

ALFRED A. KNOPF  NEW YORK

THIS IS A BORZOI BOOK PUBLISHED BY ALFRED A. KNOPF, INC.

Text copyright © 1989 by Lois Duncan and Robin Arquette
Illustrations copyright © 1989 by Kay Chorao
All rights reserved under International and Pan-American Copyright Conventions. Published
in the United States by Alfred A. Knopf, Inc., New York, and simultaneously in Canada by
Random House of Canada Limited, Toronto. Distributed by Random House, Inc., New York.

Manufactured in the United States of America   Book design by Mina Greenstein
1   3   5   7   9   10   8   6   4   2

Library of Congress Cataloging-in-Publication Data
Duncan, Lois, 1934–. Songs from dreamland : original lullabies / by Lois Duncan.   p.   cm.
Summary: An illustrated collection of lullabies and poems about sleep.   ISBN 0-394-89904-0
(trade) ISBN 0-394-99904-5 (lib. bdg.) ISBN 0-394-82862-3 (book-cassette)   1. Lullabies,
American.   2. Sleep—Juvenile poetry.   3. Children's poetry, American.   [1. Lullabies.
2. Sleep—Poetry.   3. American poetry.]   I. Chorao, Kay, ill.   II. Title.
PS3554.U464S66   1989   811'.54—dc19   88-21742

For Erin and Brittany Mahrer with love
—L.D. and R.A.

For Janet Schulman
—K.C.

WIND SONG

Wind at the window, sing us a silver song,
Silver as foam on an icy sea—
Silver as snow light,
Piercing the winter night,
Wind song and snow song for baby and me.

Wind song, silver song for us—
Sing it for baby and me.

Moon in the meadow, croon us a golden song,
Gold as the hum of the drowsy bees—
Gold as the moonlight,
Flooding the summer night,
Bee song and moon song for baby and me.

Moon song, golden song for us—
Sing it for baby and me.

Gold songs, silver songs for us—
Sing them for baby and me.

ROCKING CHAIR SONG

Somebody's baby is funny and fat—
Somebody's baby is naughty—
Somebody's baby got mad at the cat,
And somebody's baby is sorry for that.

Rock, rock–rock, rock–
Mother's rocking baby–
Rock, rock–rock, rock–
Mother's rocking baby.

Somebody's baby is bonny and bright—
Somebody's baby is funny—
Somebody's baby won't nap when it's light,
So somebody's baby gets cranky at night.

Rock, rock–rock, rock–
Mother's rocking baby–
Rock, rock–rock, rock–
Mother's rocking baby.

Somebody's baby is covered with crumbs—
Somebody's baby likes cookies—
Sooner or later the Sandman will come,
For somebody's baby is sucking a thumb.

Rock, rock–rock, rock–
Mother's rocking baby–
Rock, rock–rock, rock–
Mother's rocking baby.

WISH ON A STAR

Look out the window and wish on a star!
Wish on it quickly wherever you are.
Wish for the dream most important to you—
Wish, and that dream may come true.

Wish for a fuzzy warm kitten to hold.
Wish for a pony with hooves made of gold.
Wish for a necklace of sunbeams and dew—
Wish, and your dream may come true.

For the first star at night is a wondrous light
That is placed in the sky by the elves.
As it twinkles and gleams it can grant us our dreams,
As we know, for we've tried it ourselves—

Mommy and Daddy once wished on a star,
Wished on that magical light from afar,
Wished for a baby exactly like you—
See how our dream has come true!

THE SLEEPY SUN

When the sun is getting sleepy,
She slides down behind the trees,
Where she snuggles while she listens
To the singing of the breeze.
When my baby's getting sleepy,
He climbs up into my lap,
And he lets me sing him love songs
While he takes a little nap.

When the sun is very sleepy,
She slides down behind the hill,
Where she dozes in the shadows
While the world grows dark and still.
When my baby's very sleepy,
He leans back against my chest,
And he lets me hold and rock him
While he takes a little rest.

When the sun is *really* sleepy,
She slides down into the sea,
Where she dreams among the fishes
Of the day that's yet to be.
When my baby's *really* sleepy,
He falls fast asleep, and then,
He dreams of golden morning,
When the sun gets up again.

WHAT DID YOU DO TODAY?

What did you do today, little dog?
What did you do today?
"I went for a run on a rabbit trail.
I barked at the postman who brought the mail.
I yipped and I yapped, and I wagged my tail,
And that's what I did today."

Good night, little dog. Good night, little dog.
You have done everything right, little dog.
And now it is time to sleep tight, little dog,
For you've had a busy day.

What did you do today, little cat?
What did you do today?
"I purred so hard that my throat got sore.
I cleaned up a spill from the kitchen floor.
I got in a fight with the cat next door,
And that's what I did today."

Good night, little cat. Good night, little cat.
You have done everything right, little cat.
And now it is time to sleep tight, little cat,
For you've had a busy day.

What did you do today, little child?
What did you do today?
"I played in the car while we rode downtown.
I played in the park till the sun went down.
I played in the bath till the washrag drowned,
And that's what I did today."

Good night, little child. Good night, little child.
You have done everything right, little child.
Now I will snuggle you tight, little child,
For it's been a busy day.

TUCKING-IN SONG

Just one drink of water
Is all you will get.
With two drinks of water,
The bed might be wet.
With three drinks of water,
And one swallow more,
You'll find yourself swimming
Right out through the door.
So one drink of water–please, don't gulp that water–
One small cup of water, and not a drop more.

MOMMY'S TIRED TONIGHT

Baby, baby, loves to watch the moon,
Rising, rising, like a gold balloon.
Baby, baby, with your eyes so bright,
Close your eyes–close your eyes–
Mommy's tired tonight.

Baby, baby, loves the night bird's song,
Listens, listens, to it all night long.
Baby, baby, morning songs are best–
Go to sleep–go to sleep–
Mommy needs her rest.

Baby, baby, you've been changed and fed.
Baby, baby, see the pretty bed.
Hold your blankie, dream a happy dream–
If you don't go to sleep,
Mommy's going to scream.

Go to sleep–go to sleep–
Dream a happy dream.

DREAM ME AN APPLE TREE

Sleep, little child, and dream for me,
Dream me a white-plumed apple tree
All abloom in the early spring–
Dream me a song to sing.

Dream me a horse with a wild white mane,
Dream me a bird with a purple train,
Dream me a fish in a silken sea–
Dream me an apple tree.

Fresh from a land where dreams are made,
Tired child rests in a tree's cool shade,
Blossoms float in a silver stream—
Dream me a springtime dream.

Sleep, little child, and dream for me,
Dream me a house in an apple tree,
White lace ceiling and grass-green floor—
Dream me a child once more.

RED BIRD

Bright red bird on the branch above,
Hush your squawks and your "Peep, peep, peep."
Sing a song for the child I love—
Then fold your wings and sleep.

Brown-tailed squirrel in the maple tree,
Chat, chat, chattered till darkness fell.
Off you go with a one, two, three—
Sleep well, brown squirrel, sleep well.

For I know a child who played today
A little too hard and long,
And I know a child worn out from play—
That's why I sing this song.

Tired little head against my breast,
Soft little arms that cling so tight,
Time has come now to get some rest—
Good night, my love, good night.

THE RAIN LADY

Soft in the darkness the Rain Lady comes,
Twirling her hair with the tips of her thumbs—
Hair that is sweet as a summertime dream,
Studded with raindrops that sparkle and gleam,
Hair that is gray as the mists of the sea,
Whirling and swirling and tumbling free—
Shush, shush, don't make a sound—
Rest while the rain comes down.

Soft in the darkness the Rain Lady stands,
Shaking her hair with her gentle white hands.
Chipmunks and rabbits and ferrets and moles,
Tiny wet field mice run into their holes,
Sheep on the hillside and lambs on the plain,
Little wool blotters that soak up the rain—
Shush, shush, don't make a sound—
Rest while the rain comes down.

Soft in the darkness the Rain Lady sings,
Voice that is cool as the winds of the spring.
Rain in the leaves makes a whispering sound,
Light as the silk of the Rain Lady's gown.
Rain on the roof makes a patter like drums.
Soft in the darkness the Rain Lady comes—
Shush, shush, don't make a sound—
Rest while the rain comes down.

SLEEPY TOWN

Close your eyes–settle down–
That's how we get to Sleepy Town.
Close your eyes–settle down–
That's how we get to Sleepy Town.

Think of the wind blowing far and free,
Teasing the waves as it skims the sea.

Think of a meadow where silken grass
Bows to the wind as it hurries past.

Think of the birds in the autumn sky,
Sailing like kites when the wind goes by.

Think of the wind in the trees above,
Calling the name of the child I love.

Close your eyes—settle down—
Ride with the wind to Sleepy Town.
Close your eyes—settle down—
Ride with the wind to Sleepy Town.

THE TRAINS TO DREAMLAND

The first train bound for Dreamland
Is revving up to go.
See the sleepy passengers
Standing in a row.
Some of them are tall and thin,
Some of them are stout,
And see the silly baby
With his jammies wrongside out.

The first train bound for Dreamland
Is chugging down the track—
Mama will be waiting
When the train comes back.

The second train to Dreamland
Is standing at the gate.
See the sleepy passengers
Helping load the freight—
Baby dolls to cuddle with,
Teddy bears to pet,
And lots of fuzzy blankets
With their corners sopping wet.

The second train to Dreamland
Is chugging down the track—
Mama will be waiting
When the train comes back.

The last train bound for Dreamland
Is getting set to start.
See the sleepy passengers
Ready to depart.
Some are from the Northern Lands,
Some are from the South,
And see the silly baby
With her fingers in her mouth.

The last train bound for Dreamland
Is chugging down the track–
Mama will be waiting
When the train comes back.

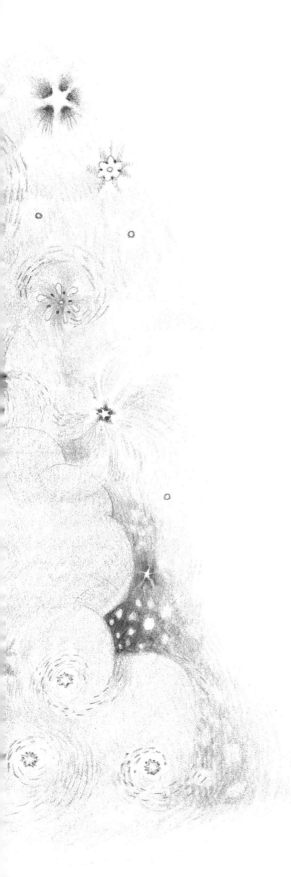

EVENING PRAYER

The beautiful day has slipped away,
And the night has moved gently in.
I kneel by my bed, and I offer thanks
For the wonderful time that has been,
For the song of the birds in the trees above
And the warmth of the golden sun.
I thank you, God, for your loving gift
Of the beautiful day that is done.

The beautiful night feels cool and right,
Now the warmth of the day is gone.
I kneel by my bed, and I offer thanks
For the wonderful hours till dawn,
For the crickets' song in the darkened hedge
While the stars fill the sky like flowers.
I thank you, God, for your loving gift
Of this beautiful night of ours.

SHIP IN THE NIGHT

Ship in the night—with salt in your sails—
Oh, what do you bring me from out of the deep?
"I bring you this wish from a magical fish—
Go to sleep. Go to sleep. Close your eyes. Go to sleep.
I bring you a comb that's frosted with foam,
A gift from a mermaid who wouldn't leave home,
And I'm bringing with me the song of the sea
To sing to the child that you love."

Ship in the night—with clouds in your sails—
Oh, what do you bring me from star-laden skies?
"A song that I heard from a magical bird—
Close your eyes. Close your eyes. Go to sleep. Close your eyes.
I've filled up my hold with gossamer gold
To weave you a blanket to keep out the cold,
And I bring you a tune I learned from the moon
To sing to the child that you love."

Lois Duncan, author of more than 30 novels for children and young adults, got the idea to write *Songs from Dreamland* when her first grandchild, Erin, who would not sleep at night, ran through the standard repertoire of "go-to-sleep" cassettes. Her eldest daughter, Robin Arquette, a professional singer and Erin's aunt, composed music to go with the lyrics. The lovely, lilting cassette *Songs from Dreamland* is the result of their collaboration.

Lois Duncan lives in Albuquerque, New Mexico, and Robin Arquette lives in Sarasota, Florida.

Kay Chorao is a fine painter who has written as well as illustrated many beautiful picture books. Her *The Baby's Lap Book, The Baby's Bedtime Book, The Baby's Good Morning Book,* and *The Baby's Storybook,* all of which are illustrated in a style similar to that of *Songs from Dreamland,* are considered outstanding books for the nursery-age child. She lives in New York City.

Just one bedtime story
Is all I will read.
For two bedtime stories
Are more than you need,
And three bedtime stories
Would take us all night;
We wouldn't be done
Till the sky filled with light.
So one bedtime story—one fairy-tale story—
One happy-end story, is all for tonight.

Just one good-night kiss
On the tip of your nose.
Then ten good-night kisses
On all of your toes.
A hundred more kisses
(That seems like so few),
There's just not enough
For a baby like you.
For kisses are different—and kisses are special—
And one good-night kiss—well, that just wouldn't do!